The
WEIR

Poems
by
Peter Dickinson

THE WEIR
A PETER DICKINSON BOOK
Paperback edition ISBN 978-0-9557805-1-6

Published in Great Britain by Peter Dickinson Books

This edition published 2007

1 3 5 7 9 10 8 6 4 2

Set in Bembo

PETER DICKINSON BOOKS
1 Arlebury Park Mews
Alresford
Hants SO24 9ER

www.peterdickinson.com

A CIP catalogue record for this book
is available from the British Library.

Printed in the UK by CPI Antony Rowe,
Chippenham, SN14 6LH

THE WEIR

All, all of our lives,
We tumble over the moment,
Ahead, unreadable ferment,
Behind, the ordered stream.
But just as the moment arrives
Notice a change in the gleam?
A patch where the light is caught
By a surface drawn silky taut
With the expectation of fall?
This is our lives, all, all.

NOTE

I've arranged the poems in four rough sequences: first, ones that I needed to write for strongly felt personal reasons, or that I felt needed to be written; second, ones written mainly to amuse myself or others, or, in a few cases, because they were commissioned; third, those written for children; finally, a sample of the four-hundred-odd poems I wrote for *Punch* in the 'fifties and 'sixties – unsurprisingly, I wrote very little else in those years. I've dated these last, as that may be of interest. The rest are in rough chronological order within their sections. I haven't given the sections titles, as none seemed appropriate, and in any case many of the poems could perfectly well have appeared elsewhere.

Walking to School first appeared in *The Week-end Telegraph*; *Infinite Loop* in *Encounter*; and *Commuters* in *The Atlantic Monthly*. Sonnet, Egdon Heath, It's an Ill Windbag, Sestina in Season, Cutting-Edge (Antimatter), Love in the Laboratory, Poultry Country, Epitaph for Mr Jiggs, The Moon is Female, "Corresponding De-escalation" and From Slum to Chic are reprinted from *Punch* by kind permission of Punch Ltd (punch.library@harrods.com).

Finally, my thanks are due to Margaret Hope and Jane Seery for the design and production of this book, and to my family for helping me to publish it in time for my eightieth birthday, and in some cases allowing me to include poems that are also personal to them.

CONTENTS

1

2

3

4

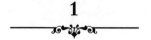

WALKING TO SCHOOL
(for Philippa and Polly)

These dolphining children skim through milder seas
Than they will measure when they've grown their span.
Kind are their rippling waves, gentle their wind,
        Their pleasures small and here.

Not that the underdeeps are free from what
We flinch at in the headlines, suddenly
Moving in obscene parody of love,
        One swirl, and the life gone.

Or, with less drama, innocence no more.
I recall Mr Clavec's soft brown eye
Shining above his seven-shilling wine.
        He grinned and asked why we

English make such a fuss about the thing.
Quoting at large, he claimed our authors wrote
Of loss of innocence as much as love.
        Wordsworth, he said, still stirred

In Dylan Thomas, Hartley's *Go-Between*,
John Betjeman – his list went on and on.
". . . No other major literature can show
        This bizarre emphasis."

"Just us, the English? What about dear old Proust?
And, of course, Rimbaud?" "Rimbaud, my dear man!
Not a Wordsworthian impetus. No, what
                    Distinguishes my list

"Is the *inevitable* theft of bliss
Seen as a loss that could, and should, have been
Escaped, by nursery magic, more or less."
                    To-day, I'm in that mood

Which Mr Clavec found so strangely rich
In contradiction. Surely, in Berlin,
Paris, perhaps, or Prague, or Rome, there are
                    Fathers who walk this path,

Who daily take their skipping children through
Their own equivalent of my strolling here
Under the planes in the faint April sun –
                    Who almost daily, too,

Get from the trip this fierce, absurd regret –
Sin (of the fathers, arguably) in
Ambush? Or really don't they give a damn?
                    Wait at the old iron gate,

.

8

Standing on adulthood's deep-layered land
To watch the shining creatures skipping through,
Pavement their ocean, time their passing wave.
                    They skip the wave away

Down worn cement steps to the green and brown
Gloom of the shrilling basement dressing room.
Change shoes. Hang coats on pegs. Kiss cheeks. Arrange
                    Hairbands. They disappear.

Myth, in all tongues, credits the dolphins with
Making the bays they visit cheerful, waking
Song in flint cottages that lacked it long.
                    Man haunts what shores he can.

INFINITE LOOP

A pine-glade, seen descending from the pass:
   A single chunk of out-at-elbows rock
Prods through the lettuce-coloured upland grass;
   Pink tree-trunks; dangling moss . . .

                        Why has it stuck
   Considering I do not even know
What holiday, which mountain-range it was?
   Or dream?

             No, not a dream. It is as though
Some fault deep in my circuitry, some block,
   Could never let the once-seen image go,
But kept repeating *rock; grass; tree-trunks; moss,*
   An unheard whisper.

                 Twice a year or so
It surfaces, bringing the same mild shock
   Of clarity, then puzzlement of loss.
Senile, in my residual bric-a-brac
   Will this one shard retain its brilliant glow?

   The road curved down in tight, exacting lines
   Between undifferentiable pines.

COMMUTERS

Drumming in warmed compartments up to town
On mornings of oboe weather through the truck-yards,
A metal desolation flowering with steam,
      It is unwise to dream,
To let the still half-drowsing mind slip backwards
To the green end of the sweatier journey down.

Though weeds disrupt the intricacies of metal
And weather rule this outer desolation
Town is stiff acres waiting for your plough,
      While fields and hedges now
For you are the furnishings of civilisation,
A world as artificial as a petal.

Think about something other than returning
Lest green dreams skew your ploughing until the street
Opens its heavy-lidded lamps. You've made
      This journey your stockade.
Live in its instant. Watch from your window-seat
The cooling towers silently brewing the morning.

WAKING AT NIGHT

It has rained again, from the hiss of tyre on tar.
And it's late, for that was the sound of a single car.
　　Yes, late. Now only the neon street-lamp sends
Its sash-shadow rhombs on the ceiling. The lights at The Star
　　Are out, long out – since Saturday evening ends
　　With hallooings of boozy good-nights from pavement-friends.

In London it's never dark. Though the room is hung
With pompous shadows, her face is vivid among
　　The shadows of loosened hair. The church strikes four.
The planes of forehead and cheek are serene and young.
　　She shifts her weight with a soft, contented snore.
　　If I wake her, that private world will exist no more.

(Oh, it's true the village kids have nowhere to play,
So mooch round the fumy garage forecourt all day.
　　Are we morally bound to let them loose in the park,
Where they'll frighten our white and tumbling doves away
　　And smash the trees, and muddy the lake for a lark?)
　　I close my eyes and summon my separate dark.

K

Grief for a lifetime somehow incomplete,
    Somehow short-changed, despite its length in years.
    Time and again her photograph appears
In other people's albums: "Athens – Pete,
K, Dave." That look, before time coarsened it,
    The young invader on the glaciers,
    Clean mountain sunlight twinkling off the spears,
The world's luxurious plain laid at her feet.

Relief that it is over, the long war.
    I knew her old, and, yes, the look still spoke,
Often, in flash of eye and tilt of jaw.
    She wrapped her myth around her like a cloak,
Looked back through misted eyes, so never saw
    Across the spoiled terrain the dwindling smoke.

REPAIRING A ROOF

All our lifetime mortal clay
Mends its substance day by day.
Other substances decay,
Rust, rot, perish, flake away.

All our lifetime we must spend
Vital energies to mend
Anything we would suspend
From the grim entropic trend.

This I, Peter, and I, John,
Through a summer month have done
That this much loved house live on
When our subtler clay is gone.

BINOCULAR VISION

We make sense through our senses, through our eyes
    Shape line and mass to landscape, so that I
May open for you, of all other "I"s,
    The gate to the rich pastures of an eye.
Yellow with sun and dung and pollen lie
    The water-meadows, and the weaving flies
Maze in the mind, make transience a lie.
    Blur-winged on blue a hunting kestrel flies.
Mine! And so yours. Yours, and in your eyes mine,
    The double vision that makes depth and meaning.
Under our noses burnished ants move mean.
    Through willowed bands of distance sight goes mining.
Ours the clean focus of the kestrel hours
And the vague, mottled levels also ours.

THESE THREE

(For J.C.M.D. on his confirmation)

The love I bring grows green and tall.
　　Seed it has been, and will be seed,
One plant within His field, where all
　　　　Must reap, if they would feed.

The hope I bring lies thin as dew,
　　Though in some light each drop may shine
With spectral brilliancies. For you,
　　　　Oh may He make it wine.

The faith it is not mine to give
　　The marrow of your bones must make
Each heartbeat of what life you live.
　　　　No wine or bread can slake

The hunger of our mortal clay,
　　Nor clay digest such drink and food
Till faith so work on them, that they
　　　　Become His body, His blood.

A CHOSEN END

Overdose

"Can you hear me, darling? Darling!" No reply.
  She lay flushed but yellow in the evening glow.
  Her angry breath came rasping to and fro.
He couldn't find her pulse. What else to try?
Over the stony, light-rejecting eye
  The eyelid that he raised fell treacle-slow.
  Why this fourth time refuse to let her go?
He actually stood and wondered why.

Love would have let her have her way, he knew,
  But he had doubts about his own position
  Should the police question him, and an inhibition
Somewhere between dishonour and tabu.
  Telling himself he was still too stunned for pain
  He went and phoned the ambulance again.

Coming round

Mumbling through drug-daze, sallow, sensual-eyed:
  "I nearly did you that time."

                 "Bloody nearly –
  The doctor says your heart stopped."

                      "Did it really?
My heart? You mean I actually died?"
"For a heartbeat, anyway."

                She smiled with pride,
  Felt for his hand and held and squeezed it, clearly
  Thinking attempted suicide was merely
Points in their game, their life-long one-a-side,

Her *v.* The World, he perforce representing
   That world – it was him that she had "nearly done".
   Now she replayed the episode as fun.
Despair stood at his elbow, unrelenting,
   But she looked so happy, so smug with her own guile,
   He had no need to force his answering smile.

Break-out

To greet with wide-spread arms the runaway,
   To hug the trembling body, bend and kiss
   The thin, taut neck as if in bridal bliss,
To laugh aloud, and let her free, and pay
The taxi, close his desk, take a holiday,
   Walk in the garden, see the clematis
   Bought for his birthday . . . Then, in the midst of this,
Choosing some least worst moment, have to say
"Darling, you can't stay here. I'll telephone
   The hospital and tell them where you are."
"Judas."
            "But darling . . ."
                           "Course, I've always known
   You'd let me down."
                        To coax her to the car . . .
Others must hear their children burn and die.
No, this was no peculiar agony.

Distances

At least, he thought, we have been close again.
   "Please take me home."
                             "Oh, darling, if I could . . ."
"Please, please."
                      "But, darling . . ."
                             "Please. I will be good."
Weeping together, wrestling to explain
To cajole reasons into the closed brain . . .
   Still, something reasonless was understood,
   Sensed through her trembling, love and trust renewed,
Though love must now express itself as pain.

He felt so to the very end. Did she?
   Hindsight reveals her heeling towards the dark,
Dwindling with distance, gaining velocity,
   A pluming flame, a chilly star, a spark,
Nothing. And nothing to plot where she had been.
So now they have infinity between.

Gratitude to chemists

Was it happiness, or only a drug-bought high?
   Twenty-three days it lasted, not quite spring
   Come round, but a sudden unseasonal blossoming,
Smiles, and an appetite, a light in the eye,
Visits and plans. Oh, think, had she chosen to die
   Without that marvellous, maybe illusory, fling,
   With only the sordid and meaningless suffering,
Only the winter years to remember her by . . .

And more. For him it is proof. So long she had known
   No future but more waste years. Do you call that choice –
Pascal's bet in reverse? But now she'd been shown
   A life in which she might even, one day, rejoice.
Who cares what caused some synapse to open, then close?
For him it is proof that there was such a choice, and she chose.

Lost planet

She was deliberate about it, conned
   His watchfulness by troubling with her hair
   And sometimes smiling. Should he have been aware?
That tremulous kiss at the door – frightened, not fond?
Not getting that much, how could he respond?
   All pockets emptied, but for a single fare,
   She'd walked to the station, taken the moving stair . . .
He would not think of anything beyond.

She was her world, a world that has swung too far
   From its centering sun. He cannot fully mourn,
      Knowing no grief that he can feel composes
Landscapes as chill as hers, years as forlorn.
   He jokes with children while he cleans the car
      But for six weeks forgets to spray the roses.

MRD

This ash to earth to keep.
Lie undisturbed, lie deep.
And, brave, loved, tortured soul,
Be nothing. Or be whole.

Letters I

So many writers use the word "serene".
  He cannot call them blind. How could they know?
  He recalls visiting good Doctor O-----,
Whose trade is knowing:

                              "Well, and how've we been?"
"F-fine, I think."

                    A buoyant tone and mien,
  A flirting tilt of the neck, almost a glow . . .
  That reticent stammer – nothing else to show
Her fiend was back, esurient, obscene.

Slim sandstone pillars against azure sky,
  Roofless and pure, are what the tourist sees.
Nothing suggests, even to the inward eye,
  The sperm-smeared priests, their grisly mysteries.
The pillars stand, proclaiming beauty true.
Can a souvenir postcard offer an opposite view?

Midden

Things he'd been begging her to bin for years –
  These loose-leaf folders clipped from magazines,
  Some of them dating right back to her teens,
Gardening notes, fish-recipes, careers
Advice, health, night-schools, travel in Algiers,
  Designs for swimming pools beyond their means,
  Home insulation – now at last he bins,
But why so reasonlessly close to tears?

As much as statues and philosophies,
  The middens of lost peoples speak their mind,
Their breakages and throw-outs. So in these
  Some inwardness of hers seems left behind.
For a few desolate instants now he sees
  Her as his breakage, sighed over, but binned.

Letters II

To whom to tell what truths? Old friends, lost touch
  With in her illness, writing to convey
  Imagined empathies, their shared dismay
And sorrow – does truth matter, now, that much?
Mostly he answers with the obvious clutch
  Of cliches, but then feels compelled to say
  She chose her death, like a toiled-for holiday.
This was *her* truth, and must be told as such.

Sometimes to almost-strangers, though, he tells
  His truth, those foreseen futures, stage by stage
Leading to too-imaginable hells.
  Love had become their ever-narrowing cage.
Despairingly he'd sought the years-lost key.
From her smashed flesh she forged one, and set him free.

Evolutionary

Their grandson on his arm, the skull still bruised
  With fighting through to birth, the nothing nose
  And blear blue eyes – he can't but think: Suppose
She'd lived these last weeks, might this not have loosed
Some missing molecule, some brain-produced
  Signal, and in that marvellous maze (who knows?)
  Unblocked a path her illness caused to close?
Might grandmothers be programmed to be used?

Life-forms evolve a bias to survive.
  Reasoning life-forms then must wonder why.
Because the truth is trivial, they contrive
  Half-truths, like love. We think we love or die.
In short, though genes may well be all we're here for,
We still need more than stupid genes to care for.

Inquest

The driver didn't come. The coroner read
  His statement, saying he was still in shock.
  He'd left White City, plunged into the dark,
Seen Shepherds Bush an arch of light ahead,
Its near lights green, the further ones still red.
  Within that arch a figure dressed in black
  Climbed down and laid its head upon the track.
He'd braked, but known it was too late, he said.

Oh those enduring seconds, with clenched teeth,
   Waiting the pain-blast. She always dreaded pain,
   But would not weep or groan, barely complain.
      Endure, endure. See through what's ill begun . . .
They switched the current off and crawled beneath
      The train, "but there was nothing to be done."

Moving house

Two sons born in this room that now stands bare,
   One into his own hands, the midwife late,
   She gasping, he staring ignorantly at
The swollen kinks of the cord. Feet on the stair
At last, and a tiny black nurse chortling there:
      "Hey! This is what we call precipitate
      Delivery! Some people just won't wait!"
   . . . Why now no ghost, no tremor in the air?

Hauntings are not like that. As you turn your head
They are gone, the sly and inconsiderate dead.
   The pang will come in some unhistoried place –
Passing a playground blotched with thawing snow,
The gesture of a stranger's child – but no,
   He will never meet her phantom face to face.

HEDGEROW TREES

Now in midwinter, every twiglet bare,
    One sees what shape the dead tree left behind,
    The side its mass of branches intertwined
With the still living of the ancient pair
In their long contest for the light and air.
    The partner too, though only half-defined
    By its own absence, hovers in the mind,
More of a presence than when standing here.

They grow to their discomforts, those thus twinned,
    As much as from the benefits they share,
And missing them seem less themselves, skewed, thinned . . .
    Now through the lone tree's hissing can I not hear
The emptiness beside it shrill in the wind?
      I am allowed to think so. I have been there.

FLINT

Two spits down, the size of a horse's head,
   And roughly that shape, though the shape of each is its own,
Fully distinct. Such a skull, turned up by the spade
   Would speak with the violent eloquence of bone,
        Crying "Was horse. Am dead."

But it wouldn't speak of any particular horse,
   Just Ideas of Horse, and Death. Whereas this stone,
Though it seems to speak with at least an equal force,
   Does so in a manner that tells of itself, alone.
        Its speech is opaque, of course,

To the human mind, but in it this flint seems a word
   Meaning "this flint", a resonant proper noun,
Loded with imports. Hm. So I claim to be stirred
   By an utterance in a tongue that cannot be known?
        Ask, and the question's absurd,

Hence the wrong question. The right one, clearly, would be
   Not to posit some fancy-engendered lithophone
And attempt to commune with its innermost mystery,
   But to acknowledge the wonder as more home grown
        And ask what is it in me

That chooses so to be stirred? I heave out the mass
  And stare at it, knowing I've done no more than postpone
The problem by shifting it to an inwardness
  Not a whit more accessible than the previous one.
      However my fingers caress

The complex surface, nothing exchanges. No flow
  Passes to or from flesh at ridge or dimple or cone –
Which is probably just as well, considering how
  The whole of this landscape with similar objects is strewn
      Below the churn of the plough.

. . . x 2

Astounding to think of the binary ancestors
Receding up that mathematical stair,
As individuals meaningless, bones under moors,
But alive in this place, each having been one of a pair,
Each pair doubling the unsummable sum,
Lover and lover, power beyond power of two . . .
Look! To your wedding the generations have come,
All those powers, in this place and this hour, in you.

Justly then we rejoice, for at such places, such hours,
Exact at the point where line intersects with line,
Remaking the timeless mathematical sign,
Energies funnel to a focus, chance becomes willed,
Moments are filled with lifetimes, themselves fulfilled . . .
You meet at the fortunate crossways. Yours are the powers.

MEME

"The corn was orient and immortal wheat, which never should be reaped,
nor was ever sown. I thought it had stood from everlasting to everlasting."
Thomas Traherne: *Centuries of Meditations*

The footpath crosses a field. That is all there is to it.
  Crop, either barley or wheat – no rotation at all
  Within the forty-odd years of my recall.
A field at the top of a ridge, with a path running through it.

Unlovely in winter, especially after a frost,
  When the half-thawed Hampshire clay clogs onto one's boots
  Inch thick, and people have trampled the wan wheat shoots
Side-stepping the worst of the mire, so the line is lost.

But come back in March, when the crop is suddenly growing.
  Our feet have decided: this time the path runs *here*.
  Not ruler-straight, but a line like a natural shear
Between leaves that arch, sway, shimmer, seem to be flowing.

Or, better, July. Now, barely a walker wide,
  A wriggling cleft runs between cliffs of stalks,
  Hip-high to an adult. One raises one's arms as one walks
Rather than rasp on the stems upon either side.

Yes, now is the moment. A stranger might sense the wonder –
  Perhaps be struck by it no less strongly than I –
  How this canyon carved by a river of passers-by
Runnels down through the surface of time into layers long under.

Combine and baler come, but the path persists,
  Sharply defined through the stubble. Then comes the plough,
  Heaving up foot-deep clods, and where is it now?
Gone from the face of the earth. But still it exists.

Stumbling we trudge the tilted ridges, taking
  Each our own route, because there is little to show
  Where whoever came next before us elected to go.
We leave no path. But then come the harrows, raking

The clods to a tilth. They scrape used parchment clean
  For the seeder to pen fresh lines. We cross with our one.
  In less than a week, unnoticed, the thing is done.
The footpath runs through its field. So where has it been?

It is marked on the earliest survey I can find,
  But that mark isn't *it*, not the actual footpath worn
  By the feet of the dead for the feet of the not yet born.
That exists, as it always has, in our communal mind,

Within which mind the crop stands always full grown,
  The path bears the print of those generations of feet,
  And we walk through the orient and immortal wheat,
Which never should be reaped, nor was ever sown.

THE INVADERS

Yes, there were histories.
Cromlech, hill-rampart, turf-maze, tumulus
(Each other's landscape we invade) declare
Lost meanings – Blood-rites? Triumphs? Obsequies?
    Opaque to us
They stand unthreatening in the summer air.

    At the other solstice, drum
And pipe, faint, far, may thread within the gales.
We'll lie in warmth and tell each other *It's*
The Old Ones, their grim fetish having become
    In nursery tales
The three-eyed giant our heroine outwits.

    Stones have no hidden power.
This basalt slab, no matter what was done
Upon it, is the hearth our ash will smother.
We calendar this noon, this shadowless hour
    As our Year One.
Begins an era altogether other.

IN BLUE HILL

The stream is dumb with ice.
Against the door a drift.
Chill. Silence. Emptiness.
Tenants' residual mess.
A closet reeks of mice.
The three-year let has left
Harsh scars and bruises, but
Faithful the roof has kept
Three winters from the loft,
Faithful the timbers sit,
Oak that was felled and cleft
Before the redcoats went.

A buyer, never met,
Is said to love the place.
May it be true, as it
Was true long since, no doubt,
For other owners, yet
You are not by that bereft.
This was and is your house
And will be, in your eyes,
Until your sun is set.
It gave itself, a gift
Like love, which you returned
As love, and both were earned.

AN EDUCATION

Always there had been signs.
As soon as she could walk alone she learned
The look of certain yellow-mottled vines
That dangled in her pathways. Touched, they burned,
    Burned rancid to the bone.
Terror and pain taught her how sense deceives,
Taught her to tell the stone-asp from the stone,
Probe for the toothed steel under littered leaves,
    And to leave ill alone.

    Later, in desert noons,
Though mirages might glisten through the blaze
She tracked faint dimplings on the unsteady dunes,
Following the timid desert creatures' ways
    To where scant water ran.
Or else by night would scan the alien sky,
Choose constellations, name them one by one,
Guess each name's meaning, thence some destiny –
    Better dark signs than none.

    And then the city. Steeple and minaret
Chimed *Welcome*, chanted *Honour*. Disciplined trees
Oozed *Law*, reeked *Decency*, while glance and gait
Of strollers in their shade spoke *Wealth, Taste, Ease,*
    Delight. But every breath
She drew, each echo of her footfall told
How in some echoing labyrinth beneath
Those statued vistas, waiting for her, prowled
    Their bestial founding myth.

So, in this garden, how
Shall inward tongues not whisper to her, taunt,
Tell her to search for signals even now,
Corrode her certainties that pool and plant
        Are simply what they seem?
And did you choose the roses? Did you tame
The brambles? And last winter cleared the stream?
Indeed? You gave the drowsing hound his name?
        What waking from such dream?

YOU ASKED WHY I LOVE YOU

        Describe the sun.
List heat, size, distance, gravitational pull
That swings the planets around it, including ours . . .
        Still you have not begun,
However subtle your list, however full,
To *describe* it, to say what it *is*, its meaning, its powers.

        We are made of the sun.
Yes, children of light. Our flesh is the bread of its baking.
All of us, muscle, bone, gland, entrail and neuron, came
        Ultimately from one
Collision of sunlight with matter. So, now, waking,
Our chilled skin crawls to its touch. We walk in its flame.

TWO ON A BED

An eddy of limbs, at its centre the dog's dark eye
   Watching me, wary, wary, as I dress.
     The woman's chin rests on the dog's curved nape,
      Her lids clenched shut beneath a puzzling frown.
       Why, when everything else so speaks of repose,
        Apart from that eye? Oh, and the eddy, of course,
        Motion in stillness, the swirl of a Celtic brooch –
        Broken, for though the whippet's flexible spine
        Can curve to a natural spiral, chin upon thigh,
        With the body coiling around that glistening eye,
        The arc of the human frame, settled comfortably,
        Incarnates only half of the outer line.
      And the missing half? The frown unspoken reproach?
      Ah, no, my dear, no late-come mishap the source
     Of such discontent. Plough-deep lie the fracture, the loss.
    Yet *something* persists in the blank that is all I'm shown
   As symmetry reconstructs the part-visible shape.
  The dog may have inklings. Me, I'd sooner not guess.
An eddy in time, at its centre a watching eye.

FIVE FINGER EXERCISE

Here. I give you my hand,
 Laying it palm down upon your scrubbed deal board.
Mauve in their delta the plump, hummocked arteries stand,
Feeding muscular fingers, each at both knuckles scored
  With skin-folds in a loose irregular band.

    Practical, used to spade
 And saw, but less, as you know too well, to the grand
Or the sensitive gesture. Could be given to someone in aid,
To acknowledge a stranger, or formally welcome a friend.
  Of such givings is the good society made.

 That hand I show. I turn it, making visible
For you its more private side – a dog's belly displayed
In submission, it is now beseeching, deliberately vulnerable,
  Dumbly demanding a some coin of affection be paid.
      My hand begs at your table.

 Thus open, my intimate oddity is revealed,
Heart line and head line joined, running straight as tow-cable
(One in some thousand people has a hand like this, I'm told)
  From palm's edge to edge. It is said to mean I'm unable
      To separate *will* from *would*.

Now I clench it into its third
 Figuration – confront or enfold.
  Skin tight over bone, stone-hard.
  Yours, given to have and to hold.
On my hand I give you my word.

THE OTHER END OF THE TELESCOPE

In memoriam Angel, Jan-Dec 2001

Creation focussed down to one dot of life,
   A drop of the primal essence, embodied Will,
Absolute Self. Seen thus, no level of grief
   Seems unfitting, and this apparently miniscule
Fleck on our lives' long complex wealth becomes,
Compacted into his instant, the sum of all sums,
All that there was, is, will be, and everywhere.
Then there was bird. Now there is songless air.

THIRD

In our community three –
You, I and We.
More than just you plus me

This Third, a thing of our making,
Animate, sentient, taking
Care in its nurture, though waking

No gene-jerk-instinct appeal
By all-but-meaningless smile,
Or frame-clenching misery-bawl.

How much more subtle our Third,
Nourished by gesture, glance, word –
As it were, quanta fired

Through our kitchen cloud-chamber, breeding
At wave-lengths beyond our heeding
Via faint and instantly fading

Traces of particles . . . what?
Think time-exposure, and it
Becomes a glimmering net,

A structure like thought in the brain,
Which, though it can never explain
The thought, nor we, thinking, attain

Any glimpse of its workings, is there,
As it must be while we breathe air,
Making us who we are.
The same with this Third we share.

Cogitamus, ergo sumus.
Tres sumus quia amamus.
May it be so till we are humus.

GROUP

Dear friends – yes, friends, though most I have scarcely met
   And some I would not recognise in the street.
   I know names, a few personal details, nicely discreet,
      And yet, and yet . . .

I think of you various ways, but often as trees,
   A small yet magical grove standing strongly together.
   Your magic is this, that you generate your own weather –
      Though not as you please.

A winter storm hurls out of somebody's past
   Screeches between her branches, wrenches her bole.
   Could she endure it if she were standing sole?
      But you filter the blast.

No, more than that. You move to it, make it your own.
   The tempest batters the grove. You shake to its shock,
   But your unseen roots interweave, they cleave to the rock.
      Though your sinews groan

You hold each other secure till the batterings ease.
   Stillness, and there you stand in your magical grove,
   A place where growth is the norm, where sap dares move . . .
      Dear friends, dear trees.

THE COST OF LIVING
(For Robin: Dedication for "The Ropemaker")

Go then, adventurer, on your vivid journey,
Though once again, of course, I cannot join you --
That is as certain as your happy ending.
The one-armed captain in the pirate harbour
Would know me in an instant for a Jonah.
No gnome would ever speak with me for witness,
Thus letting slip the spell-dissolving answer
Before you'd even heard the sacred riddle.
I, as it happens, know it from my reading,
But the blind queen would ask it in a language
Not in the syllabus of my old college,
But which your loved, illiterate nanny taught you.

No, I will stay at home and keep things going,
Conduct the altercation with the builders,
Hoe the allotment, fix the carburettor.
I'm genuinely happier with such dealings;
It isn't merely that they pass the seasons
Until I hear your footstep on the threshold.
Then I will sit and listen to your story
With a complacently benign amazement,
Believing it because it's you that tell it.
And when you've done, and I have asked my questions,
I for the umpteenth time on such homecomings
Will say what's happened to the cost of living.

THE BRIDGE

Though short the pathway seems from your close keep
   To my wide-windowed house, athwart it lies
   A canyon visible only to inward eyes.
So how to span the gulf from steep to steep?

No masoned bridge, though sacrificial blood
   Mortared its stones to stand through gale and spate,
   And now to bear the juddering semi's weight,
Could leap so clean and far across the flood.

But, if we will it, with our lighter pace,
   We'll confidently to-and-fro above
     The gulf on an airy walkway we suspend
     From slim catenaries, anchored either end
    In the common rock, cemented firm with love –
Tension and steadfastness subsumed in grace.

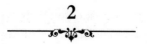

2

WHERE DO YOU GET YOUR IDEAS?

A money spider hanging in mid air.
  Like a retinal fleck it dangles from the lamp
In the blank bathroom, neither here nor there.
  You reach to take the thread. Your fingers clamp

On nothing – nothing to feel or see – and yet
  The thread is there, because the spider heaves
Beneath your hand. You take and loose it at
  The sill, to live what life a spider lives.

A symbol surely, or a metaphor
  At least. The groping mind grasps nothing. Still,
Some line of thought must have existed, for
  This fleck now dangles here, this page its sill.

SONG

If you were old and you were wise,
  As I am old and silly,
You'd know there's more than two green eyes
  From Cambridge to Caerphilly.

If you were old and you were sane,
  As I am old and foolish,
One scowl would not cause all the pain
  From Hythe to Ballachulish.

If you were old and you were cool,
  As I am old and shaken,
You would not be my kind of fool.
  But you would be mistaken.

Dear child, these worn lungs' wheezing sighs,
  This frail heart's frenzied drumming,
They drown those steps the old and wise
  Hear always coming, coming.

INSTANT

Bird or blown leaf? Quick!
There! Before seen, flip of a wing,
And gone. Wren. (Was it?)

CHRISTMAS PARTY

(after e.e.cummings)

oh
to
foxtrot with doctor
oxshott in my cocktail frock, to . . .
oh
to
kiss (quick, quick) with mister
niblick (bit of a stick) neath the mystic
mistletickletoe . . .
oh, oh, oh,
though
the
parents stare and
(dear, dear) glare in despair and . . .
oh
to
go
it
(quick, quick) with dick (dick's a
brick) in my cocktail
frock till the clock-
work (wind it quick, dick, quick)
goes . . .
oh . . . oh . . . oh . . . .
slooooow . . .
OH!

GRAVY

The gravy that made England great
Does not go sluicing round the plate,
But flows by glacial degrees
Yet does not literally freeze.
In generous servings it will hide
Spuds boiled with legless things inside,
Beef more than adequately roast
And cabbage stewed to cabbage-ghost.

   Unlike French sauces, rich in wine,
That tend to rot the moral spine,
It is not flavoured to a fault
But tastes, if anything, of salt;
So does not spoil the conversation
With little gasps of admiration,
Leave alone sending for the cook,
A custom that I will not brook.

   Since gravy of this noble sort
Was served at great King Edward's court,
So should it be today. In short,
No preparation is as good
For life, or death, or treacle pud.

MOTTO FOR ARTISTS

Perfection? There is no such stuff.
But good enough is not enough.

READING IN THE BATHROOM

Self in its tower room, instinctive Thing
   Does its task as our whippet might – easy as breathing
   In her case, the four feet gathered, on minimal earthing
   Balanced, a sculptor's posture (if doing something –
   And merely to voice the thought wakes laughter or loathing –
   Other than having a shit), a desktop plaything . . .

   Self descends from the tower, as fingers adjust my clothing,
   And settles back into Thing, rich-laden, berthing
   At the whispering quay, odours of landfall wreathing
   Decking and shrouds, home after furthest forthing,
   And only now do I notice, thrillingly soothing,
   Softly ecstatic, the physical radiance bathing
   My inwardness.
            How come I remember nothing,
  Not a single moment of the event bequeathing
This afterglow, my home-made present from Thing?

FOR AN OLD MAN'S SUNDIAL

   How slow the hours. How swift the years.
   Time lags, sags, drags, and disappea

DEMOLISHING A CUPBOARD

Crouched between shelves, like a burglar under a bed,
I wrench at the rotten timbers over my head.
    They still smell faintly of pine, some long-felled, tall,
Resinous forest. Great chunks of the house are decayed
Though my great-grandfather planned that the mansion he'd mad
             Should outlast us all.

He and the rector designed the place, over their port,
Assuring themselves that they had no need to resort
    To an architect, as all they intended to build,
Before the wine got to work, was an orthodox
Red, rectangular, mid-Victorian box.
             But glasses were filled

And emptied. Now my great-grandfather chose
To treat himself to a couple of porticos
    In classical style. The lamp was trimmed. The fire
Settled. The empty decanter was replaced.
And the rector gave rein to his passionate Gothic taste,
             Which accounts for the spire.

Flinging out wings to make room for their fancies, restrained
By neither knowledge nor taste, they entertained
    All sorts of unlikely angles unawares,
Chose oak for the paneled furlong of corridors
That ramble around these lunatic-leveled floors,
             Oak for the stairs

And the cupboards. Of course they were cheated while
The builder assembled their phantasmagoric pile.
    That's why this cupboard is deal, and rotten, what's more.
But if great grandfather was visited by a doubt
The rector came over and helped him to drive it out
                    With the '34.

Now I have their architectural hangover. Still,
This might have been oak, so I bear them no ill-will
    Shifting good oak would take stronger sinews than mine.
They left me some hellish problems, but now and again
I find myself grateful that the old gentlemen
                    Liked a glass of wine.

DINNER PARTY BLUES

    Lucky are they, beyond earth's common lot,
    Whose friends are fun, whose enemies are not.

AUBADE

The little god who guards our clock,
Whose tuts we hear as tick and tock,
Composed his visage to a frown
At ten past ten when we lay down.
How much too soon, it seemed he said,
For serious folk to get to bed.

And now, at twenty after eight,
Patently thinking it too late
For us to be still idling here,
His aspect's a disdainful sneer.
The lights were out. He has not seen
What pleasant work was done between.

CHATEAU DUCRU BEAUCAILLOU 1918

This senatorial stuff was harvested
    By wives and grandfathers and children when,
    Out on the Western front, that last young men
In France were being pricked to join the dead.
Emotion is the enemy of taste.
    Dead harvesters do not affect the wine.
    '16, for instance, managed to combine
Vintage and carnage in one classic waste.

What right has anybody got to drink it
  Who wasn't there? Well, it is in its prime,
    Polleny, dark, remarkable. What's more,
Henceforth it will be dying all the time.
  I swill and swallow. Strange indeed I think it
    That this is what the grapes were gathered for.

SOME STEAM-AGE PUBLISHERS

All night, from hush of thrush till rouse of rooster
Simon and Schuster, Simon and Schuster, Simon and Schuster,
  The great expresses thundered through my dream;
Or else on gradients more steeply canted
They *Houghton Mifflin, Houghton Mifflin* panted;
  Or the implacable wheels took up the theme;
Lippincott, Lippincott, Lippincott, they'd clink,
Lippincott, Lippincott, Doubleday and Company Inc,
  Lippincott, Lippincott, till I could scream.
I fled to British books for my salvation.
The Rationalist Press Association
  Now all night long lets off its antique steam.
And all night long a shunted freight train clanks
GOLLANCZ, *GOLLANCZ, Gollancz, Gollancz, Gollancz.*

51

3

THE SCAPEDOG

The Scapedog is a beast of sin,
    A villain of the deepest die,
But if you chance to find one in
    A pet shop, grab your purse and buy!
He'll wreck your house, but never fuss.
He's wicked for the rest of us.

He'll steal Dad's supper, gnaw Mum's hats,
    Bark like a fiend at 3 a.m.
He'll rid the neighbourhood of cats.
    Postmen? You've seen the last of them.
But all the family (behold!)
Will suddenly be good as gold.

I knew a charming family –
    So kind, so sane, such fun – who had
A scapedog for a pet, and he
    Was extra-double-record bad
They felt too good for such a scamp
And gave him to a passing tramp.

Next day that sweet and charming mother
    Wrote three rude letters to the Pope.
Papa held up some bank or other.
    The children took a piece of rope
And rustled Mrs Twitchet's cow.

The tramp's become a bishop now.

THE BARROW-MOUND

Reason is king, but still
  Beyond wait mysteries.
Under the man-piled hill
  A burial lies,
Bones that obeyed one will,
  Skull that had eyes.

Eyes frowning at the stars,
  Curious to mark
The erratic path of Mars –
  Then just a nameless spark –
Will to attempt to parse
  The grammar of the dark.

Since no historian
  Knows at what date,
Dim as the future, man
  First linked the great,
Cold, glittering night-span
  With human fate,

What harm is it to guess
  This barrow-king
Discerned in randomness
  Such patterning
And earned his burial place
  By that one thing?

What if the thing was wrong?
　He was well called wise
In his own time, who on
　The chance-strewn skies
Imposed in myth and song
　Vast destinies.

King Reason lies below
　Just such a mound,
Man-piled. How, Such and So –
　All we have found,
All that we think we know –
Bury his dry bones, though
Star-worlds of mystery glow
　Beyond, beyond.

MERLIN'S SON

They found him in the kitchen. Faint blue smoke
   Rose from his skillets. Lords of field and tower
Stood robed and ranked before him. No one spoke.
   They knew his parentage and sensed his power,
      Power never used or fee'd,
Hoarded against this single ultimate need,
      For this one hour.

They waited. He had read their mind, they knew.
   They had fought long and hard, yet all could see
Night poised to flood the realm. What would he do?
   Channel the lightning, shake the heaven-tree,
      Or wake the mighty dead?
He turned a shark-steak, glanced at them, and said
      "Let be. Let be."

POOR UNLUCKY LUCY

"Oi! Lucy! Quit your dreamin', girl. You never does a turn!
  "It's time you learned there's more to life that sittin' lookin' pretty,
"A-dreamin' of fine gennelmen. The cream is in the churn,
  "So make and take the butter now, and sell it in the city."
      Poor unlucky Lucy! Wasn't that a pity!

Close by the road as leads to town a huggly robber lay.
  'e lay, unlucky gennelman, upon a nest of hants.
So 'e 'adn't time for robbery when Lucy passed that way --
  'e was ragin' round stark naked, like, a-shakin' out 'is pants.
      Poor unlucky Lucy! Dreamin' of romance.

As Lucy stopped to gaze upon this hinteresting sight,
  Crash! in the road a'ead of 'er a rotten ellum dropped --
A wicked tree old ellum be, and chancy with it -- right
  Bang in the place where Lucy might of been, unless she'd stopped!
      Poor unlucky Lucy! Nearly you was copped!

In climbing through this hobstacle 'er cotton skirt she tore,
  Hexposin' of 'er petticoat, a gracious shade of red.
And there was Farmer Boothroyd's bull! And red it was 'e saw!
  'e pawed the ground! 'e broke 'is rope! 'e charged! 'ow Lucy fled!
      Poor unlucky Lucy! Now you're good as dead.

She fled as quick as winkin' to the bridge across the river,
  And the bull come quick be'ind 'er, and 'e was of monstruous weigh
When 'e stamped upon the timbers, why, the bridge began to shiver.
  And it broke! And they fell through it! And the river was in spate!
      Poor unlucky Lucy! What an 'ijjus fate!

The bull falls in the river, like, but Lucy in a boat,
    For 'ere comes this fine young gennelman a-puntin' on the stream,
When down into 'is arms there falls a crimson petticoat
    Containin' one young lady what's as pretty as a dream.
        Poor unlucky Lucy! Should of 'eard 'er scream!

"Ow, Lady in red petticoats, now will you be my bride?
    "For never till this moment did my 'eart feel Cupid's sting.
"I ham the Duke of Dumbleshire. My lands are rich and wide.
    "There'll be pearls upon your weddin' dress and di'monds in your ring."
        Poor unlucky Lucy! 'opin' for a king!

You'll 'ave to tell yourselves the rest. My tale goes on for hours,
    And just the same the 'ole way through, cos Lucy's made that way.
'owever full 'er life is of hexcitement, wealth and flowers,
    She thinks about what might of been and sighs "Alackaday!"
        Poor unlucky Lucy! Only 'uman clay.

NAMING THE ANIMALS

Adam said to Eve
"Oh, who and what are these
In the shadow of the trees?
This with its coarse fur,
This with its hoarse purr,
    On the young green grass?
This with its feather wings,
This with its leather wings,
In the shadow of the trees
    On the young green grass,
        The young green grass of Eden?"

"Adam," answered Eve,
"The names of these are these
In the shadow of the trees.
This is camel, this is cat,
This is bird and this is bat
    On the young green grass.
I have given each its name
Now you must do the same
In the shadow of the trees
    On the young green grass,
        The young green grass of Eden."

"Adam," wondered Eve,
"So who and what are these
In the shadow of the trees?
This with its wide jaws,
This with its white claws,
    On the young green grass?
This with its great legs,
This with its eight legs,
In the shadow of the trees
    On the young green grass,
        The young green grass of Eden?"

"Adam," answered Eve,
"The names of these are these
In the shadow of the trees.
These are crocodile and tiger,
These are elephant and spider
    On the young green grass.
We have given each its name.
May our children do the same
In the shadow of the trees,
    On the young green grass,
        The young green grass of Eden."

Beast said to beast
"But who and what are these
In the shadow of the trees?
These with their quick minds,
These with their slick lines
    On the young green grass?
Making us their game
And giving each a name
In the shadow of the trees,
    On the young green grass,
            The young green grass of Eden?"

Beast answered beast
"This, alas, are these
In the shadow of the trees --
This is man and this is woman.
They are other. They are human
    On the young green grass.
And their pride it will betray us
And their children use and slay us
In the shadow of the trees
    On the young green grass . . .
            But nevermore the grass of Eden."

BALLAD

A word of power
                    my mother taught me
When I was a lassie
                    beside her knee.
A word of power
                    my mother taught me
And told me its uses
                    one, two, three.

I sent my chosen
                    a ring of silver
And wrote within it
                    my mother's word
A day and a night, and
                    he sent in answer
A golden cage
                    for my singing bird.

I looked in my heart and
                    I looked in my mirror
And sent my chosen
                    my chamber key.
Through the dreary midnight
                    I lay wide waking
But never a footstep
                    came stealing to me.

To my bird I whispered
             the word of my mother
And loosed it forth
             in the morning dew.
When the west was crimson
             it perched at my window
And sang so sweetly
             "Your love's untrue."

I cried aloud
             the word of my mother.
Through the evening shadows
             O swift it sped.
In the dreary midnight
             a man came riding
And called at my window
             my love was dead.

O mother mine,
             my curse be upon you
For the word you taught me
             beside your knee,
The word you taught me
             when I was a lassie,
And each of its uses,
             one, two, three.

FULL CIRCLE

A thousand leagues beyond Beyond
  (Further than Far, nearer than Here)
The last magician breaks his wand
  And shapes the splinters to a star.

Then, leaning at the door of Death,
  With his last power he lights a spark,
Breathes on it with his dying breath,
  And leaves it flaming in the dark.

A planet circles round that star
  Where life evolves, and men who learn
The secretest of things, and are
  Mighty magicians in their turn.

A thousand ages pass. Their sun
  Begins to die. Their wizard skill
Makes hideous weapons. One by one
  They hunt and slay each other, till

A thousand leagues beyond Beyond
  (Further than Far, nearer than Here)
The last magician breaks his wand
  And shapes the splinters to a star.

4

SONNET

Scorn not the sonnet on the sonnet, critic.
   It is a bank where poets love to lie
   And praise each other's ingenuity
In finding such a form. The analytic
Reader may stigmatise as parasitic
   This mirror-image of a mystery,
   This echo of sweet voices, find it dry
And intellectually paralytic.

Yet 'tis a child of fancy, light and live,
   A fragile veil of nature, scarcely worn.
(Of Wordsworth's two, of Shakespeare's none, survive.)
   Empty not then the vials of scorn upon it.
   Nor, since we're on the subject, should you scorn
The sonnet on the sonnet on the sonnet.

                             1952

THOMAS HARDY ON EGDON HEATH

(Proposed as a site for a nuclear power station)

Upon the heath so long ago.
  So long ago,
The ling beneath the west wind's flow
   Would sough me, tongue-sere, small,
"Look not for purpose, sense or troth
Within the Will that planned our growth
And death. The wind and we are both
  Drab haps, and that is all."

New dooms decree that whispering,
  That whispering,
Must drown beneath the roar and ring
   Of squat, hill-shouldering tractors
And kestrels scry the heathland dour
Erupt in cooler, stack and tower
To house in salamandrine power
  The daedal-tubed reactors.

There then will purr the dynamos,
  The dynamos,
"In nescientness our current flows,
  Unfraught with good or ill.
We murmur 'neath the wind of man,
That gusts responsive to no plan
Wherein nor faith nor sense may scan
  The workings of a Will."

1956

CUTTING EDGE

In Berkeley, Cal a don
  Is making anti-matter,
No sooner made than gone,
  So fast its fragments scatter.

But, reader, do not sniff
  Or ask him why he bother. Is
The task not worth it if
  It raises this hypothesis?

That, where man's furthest sight
  The depths of space can scan, it
Is possible there might
  Exist an anti-planet.

No laws of physics ban
  That on it there should be
An anti-Cal, with an-
  ti-university,

Where, amid abstruse chatter,
  A clever anti-don
Is busy making matter,
  No sooner made than gone.

1958

SESTINA IN SPRING

When it all started, and the omnipotent gesture
Planted the Garden of Eden green in its setting
Of typical Middle Eastern desert, all
That *Genesis* tells us says nothing about the season,
But it takes some months for an apple to grow on a tree
Which makes one inclined to believe it may have been spring.

Something is always *going* to happen in spring
(As it was in Eden.) I don't mean Nature's gesture
Of leafing through the country, tree by tree,
But the all-pervasive, curiously upsetting
Whiff of the future in the uneasy season.
It is worse when nothing happens after all.

Crises can come at Christmas; so far, all
World Wars kick off in the autumn; summer can spring
A pretty fair surprise; at any season
The Chancellor can drown with the popular gesture
Of a penny off beer the noise of his taxmen setting
Their cruel taxes into some family tree.

The Fall, of course, came in the fall, if the Tree
Of Knowledge obeyed mere natural laws at all –
Which makes one think of it in an English setting
With yellow elm leaves floating on the spring
And barer branches visibly starting to gesture
Beneath the wind that sweeps away the season.

In spring, though, something *will* happen. One must season
One's natural feelings with hope. As the axle-tree
Of the year creaks over, luck may possibly gesture
This way for once. The love-child, shunned by all,
Fingers at panelling, touches a secret spring,
And lo! not one gold egg, but the whole setting.

But if it is disaster, even our setting
Cultures might find a meaning this last season,
As the beast we fathered flexes for the spring.
In much the same way that a falling tree,
After an age of pastoral bugger-all,
Discovers finally the tragic gesture.

And you, sir, digest your food; eschew upsetting
Thoughts, if you think at all; spend a sober season;
 And never climb a tree, not even in spring.

1957

LOVE IN THE LABORATORY
(For Messrs. Masters and Johnson)

"Come, let us make love deathless,
    Thou and I."
I breathe into the breathless
    Air one sigh,
A sigh at once recorded,
Analysed, measured, hoarded . . .
Ah, not for ours the sordid
    Death loves die.

Marble will fall to pieces,
    So will bronze,
Before the learned thesis
    Of these dons,
Which shows in graph and figure
How fast my passion's vigour
Contrives, dear heart, to trigger
    Your response.

Fleeting, infinitesimal,
    Look, sigh, touch
In the enduring decimal
    Foil time's clutch.
Beyond oblivion's drowning
Lives love's impassioned crowning.
Could Mrs Barrett Browning
    Say as much?

                              1958

POULTRY COUNTRY, BEFORE DAYBREAK

With a noise like creaking machinery, far away
    Over the mechanized miles of farming land,
The last free cock in the country anticipates day,
    Though the world is dark, except in chicken-huts planned
For an artificial daylight, to make hens lay
    A few more eggs by stimulating a gland.
Do those hens rejoice? Do their listless, almost grey
    Wattles stir at the cock's primeval command?
Only an agroscientist could say
    After a series of costly experiments, and
He'd only do them if he thought it might possibly pay
    (As measured in bird/feed/eggs) to have cockcrow canned
For poultry-farmers with tape-recorders to play
    To their close-caged hens.
                                    I wish I could understand
Why the thought of it keeps me from sleep until England wakes
To its flavourless eggs and ten-time-processed flakes.

                                                    1963

EPITAPH FOR MR JIGGS

"Mr Jiggs, the orang-utan at Regents Park zoo,
died yesterday, having amused thousands." *Daily Telegraph*

Monboddo believed the orang-utang was human,
  Had a sense of honour, knew how to play the flute,
And differed from us only in perfect manners,
                    And in being mute.

But Mr Jiggs sat in his iron compartment,
  A hill of indigo flesh and gingery hair,
And answered the stares of the peanut-happy people
                  With a soft brown stare.

In youth he would clown for his visitors, but later
  Grew indolent and dangerously surly,
And died of heat-stroke in his seventeenth summer,
                  For an orang, early.

What a piece of work is man, that he should imprison
  This wild, magnificent, human-seeming brute
For all those years in a desolation of boredom
                  And consider him cute.

                         1963

THE MOON IS FEMALE
(The first close-up photographs)

Full of unearthly promise she,
    Far down sight's narrowing avenue,
    Summoning and exciting, who
Turns out ('twas ever thus) to be
    A different thing on closer view,
Richly endowed with pock and pimple,
    Porridge in texture and in hue,
                And a bit simple.

And shall men cough and turn away,
    Uneasily pretending that
    They've chased a solar-wind-blown hat,
And then live out their after-day
    Whining that life is stale and flat?
Does it not rather more behove 'em
    To fling their sperm of spacecraft at
                That barren ovum?

She is in reach. The stars are not.
    So think how fortunate we are
    To shout our triumph, and hurrah
Over each wrinkle, pit and spot
    Before they grow familiar.
Also before she bears the traces –
    The mile-wide bruise, the league-long scar –
                Of Man's embraces.

                       1966

IT'S AN ILL WIND-BAG

"Sir, -- If only half of the energy the country at present devotes to the eternal discussion on sex, the pill and kindred subjects were diverted to the industrial field, our economic troubles would vanish overnight."

Letter in *Daily Telegraph*.

The wood was dark, the grass was green.
Love, both impassioned and serene,
Sang its wild note from eye to eye.
But before sigh could answer sigh
There moved across the trance-held glade
Not one, but many a hideous shade.
　A ghostly priest intoned "Fulfill
　Your human nature as you will.
　All other laws I count as nil."
　A moderator took this ill.
　His words were drowned by voices shrill
　Counting the virtues of the pill.
　A columnist was booming still
　That sex is an athletic skill
When home those luckless lovers went
Leaving the luscious grass unbent.

Drab Monday claimed its slaves again
To ease awhile the lovers' pain.
The churning lathe, the booming belt,
Unquestioning, to ends unfelt
Moved (so they thought) serene and free
From all the ills of punditry.

But round about the workshop floor
Gibbered the dreadful shades once more.
Needless to tell you what they said.
In fairness I record instead
Production rose with one huge clatter
To drown their paralyzing chatter.   1966

"CORRESPONDING DE-ESCALATION"

Come, let us meditate upon
The language of the Pentagon.
It lacks both elegance and ease.
Its name, of course, is Pentaguese.
Each general, or pentagogue,
Lives in so strange a verbal fog
Only the trained pentologist
Can hope to penetrate the mist
And tell how near is the abysm,
The dreadful, final pentaclysm.

The optimists, pentiloquent,
Measure in pent and kilopent
How great a power for good such might is.
Maybe they're suffering from pentitis.
The timid fear for hearth and home.
To them the world's a pentadrome
Where our sole safety seems to be
Emergency pentectomy.

And who is right? We have seen plenty
Of foolish, costly *pentimenti*,
But human instinct still insists
That on the whole pentagonists
Mean well. So what is crazier
Than smothering in pentaphasia
Their honest purpose and intent?
Perhaps in time they will repent.

(If you have views about Vietnam
Send LBJ a pentagram.)   1966

FROM SLUM TO CHIC
Order to View
Like a mouthful of rotten teeth
  The appalling terrace stood.
  Inside, the worm-riddled wood
Gave to our tread beneath
The worn, brown lino. The smell
  Of poverty, age and dirt
  Followed us round. A spirt
Of powdery plaster fell
At times from the lamp-blackened ceilings.

  Could we conceive of this mess
  Becoming our home? Well, yes.
This was no time for such feelings
  Or parents sighing "Oh, Lord!"
  This was what we could afford.

75

Neighbours' Voices

The landlords gradually eased
  The tenants out from either side.
Some they bribed and some they squeezed,
  And one (to do them justice) died.

Over the shallow garden wall
  We often used to lounge and speak.
With shining eyes they'd whisper all
  Each other's secrets every week:

That Mrs Gardner's sister's son
  Was out again, but not for long.
That Mr. Rogers thought he'd won
  A dividend, but got it wrong.

They didn't love their neighbours much.
  Their bent was rather more for hating.
But all were *people*, and as such
  They found them wholly fascinating.

They all knew all the others knew.
  They thought us menacing, but funny.
One subject only was tabu:
  They never spoke a word of money.

Now we have privacy. The trellises
  Are thick that screen us from the Burys
And also from the Porter-Ellises
  Beneath their ornamental cherries

We hear their voices, loud and keen,
   Telling their secrets without shame,
As if no sound could pierce the screen.
   Unconsciously we do the same.

Odd that we all of us should speak
   Only of what we truly care for:
What Number 7 fetched last week,
   And what *our* house would go for therefore.

The Last of the Old Guard

Regular, every night about eight o'clock
   Old Mrs. Storey would bang on the party wall.
      I'd fetch my torch and go unwillingly round.
In a fumbling clatter of keys she would then unlock
   Every room, and I would inspect them all,
      Flashing my torch around. But I never found

A single intruder. At first I thought the old dear
   Was scared. She shivered. Her eyes were diamond-bright
      As the shaft of light swung through the chill, damp gloom
And showed her each shadow was honestly totally clear
   Of the species of thug who might have gone thunk in the night.
      She sighed (I thought with relief) as she locked each room.

As the weeks wore on I changed my mind. I decided
   That this was her hour of excitement in the day.
      She shivered and sighed as she hung from the frightful cliff
(Pearl White at eighty) but worried much less than I did.
   At last her nephew came and took her away
      To a bright new flat. I hope she wasn't bored stiff.

Grady Singing

A crowd of Irish used the pub
Partly as rough-house, partly club.
At closing time on Saturday nights
Their shrilling women watched the fights.
Smashed glass would tinkle onto stone;
Bone thudded aimlessly on bone;
And we, two storeys overhead,
Safe in the castle of our bed,
Would hear the strange and dangerous sea
Of working-class humanity
Threshing along our cosy shores.
Then, suddenly, the shrieks and roars
(On lucky nights) would die away –
Grady was singing *Galway Bay*.

It's hard to convey his singing,
    A tenor, briny but sweet,
Harsh but effortless, ringing
    Along the prosaic street.

We'd lie in the darkness hearing
    Him bounce his voice off the walls,
While down there, under the staring
    Neon, rapt from their brawls,

The homesick Irishmen, jamming
    The pavement, stood to enjoy
The echoes of Grady slamming
    The Wild Colonial Boy

Over our moonlit tiling.
  Then with lilting pathos he'd do
When Irish Eyes are Smiling.
  He never sang anything new.

He might have kept us from sleeping
  Through the livelong darkness, but
He'd lie in the gutter weeping
  When the drink was out of his gut.

The fights resumed as they'd begun
Till cops arrived to stop the fun.

On Saturday nights *The Plough*
Has different customers now:
Taut little blondes in beads;
Men in blazers or tweeds;
The occasional polo-necked
Asserting an intellect;
A would-be baritone braying,
Perhaps, with a pianist playing
Numbers from *My Fair Lady*.
It made me ask after Grady.
"The singer?" the landlord said.
"I think I heard that he's dead."

                                    1967

PALINODE

Surely the quack must yearn just once to heal,
The falsest prophet hanker to reveal.
And should the poetaster still refuse
To hope The Mews has welcomed in the Muse?